700031651503

Guy Fawkes

Dereen Taylor

First published in 2007 by Wayland

Copyright © Wayland 2007

Wayland
338 Euston Road
London NW1 3BH

Wayland Australia
Level 17/207 Kent Street
Sydney, NSW 2000

All rights reserved.

Editor: Victoria Brooker
Designer: Jane Stanley

WORCESTERSHIRE COUNTY COUNCIL	
150	
Bertrams	17.02.08
JB FAWKES,G	£11.99
BV	

Taylor, Dereen
  Who was Guy Fawkes?
  1. Fawkes, Guy, 1570-1606 - Juvenile literature
  2. Gunpowder Plot, 1605 - Juvenile literature 3. Great
  Britain - History - James I, 1603-1625 - Juvenile
  literature
  I. Title
  942'.061'092
ISBN 978 0 7502 5194 5

Printed in China
Wayland is a division of Hachette Children's Books, an Hachette Livre UK Company.

For permission to reproduce the following pictures, the author and publisher would like
to thank: Art Archive: 8, 20; Ashmolean Museum, University of Oxford, UK/Bridgeman
Art Library, London: 17; Bibliotheque Nationale, Paris, France/Archives Charmet/
Bridgeman Art Library, London: 9; Mary Evans Picture Library: 12; Getty Images
(Hulton Archive): 4, 14, 16, 18, 19, Cover; Stirling Maxwell Collection, Pollock House,
Glasgow, Scotland/©Glasgow City Council/Bridgeman Art Library: 10; ©Toby
Melville/Reuters/Corbis: 21; Private Collection/Archives Charmet/Bridgeman Art
Library, London: 11; Private Collection/Stapleton Collection/Bridgeman Art Library,
London: 13; Roy Rainford/Robert Harding World Imagery: 5; St Faith's Church,
Gaywood, Norfolk, UK/Bridgeman Art Library, London: 15; Steve Sant/Alamy
Images: 7; ©2006 Alinari/TopFoto.co.uk: 6

The website addresses (URLs) included in this book were valid at the time of going to
press. However, because of the nature of the Internet, it is possible that some addresses
may have changed, or sites may have changed or closed down since publication. While
the author and Publisher regret any inconvenience this may cause the readers, no
responsibility for any such changes can be accepted by either the author or the Publisher.

Contents

Words in **bold** can be found in the glossary.

Who was Guy Fawkes?

Over 400 years ago, Guy Fawkes was a member of a gang who tried to blow up the **Houses of Parliament**. The plan was to kill James I, the king of England.

An engraving of Guy Fawkes.

The plan was called the Gunpowder Plot and it was due to take place on 5 November 1605. Guy Fawkes' role in the plan was to light the **explosives**. But he was caught before he could carry out this very important job.

The Houses of Parliament today are very different from those of 400 years ago. They were rebuilt after a fire in 1834.

Guy's childhood

Guy was born in Stonegate, York in 1570. His family were **Protestants** and Guy was **christened** in the Church of Saint Michael-le-Belfry in York.

This photograph of Stonegate was taken in around 1880. The style of buildings and cobbled streets are similar to when Guy lived there 300 years before.

When Guy was nine, his father died and his mother got married again to a **Catholic**. Elizabeth I was queen at that time. She was Protestant and wanted everyone else to be Protestants too. Catholics had to practise their religion in secret.

Some people hid Catholic priests in secret places in their homes to keep them safe.

Places to Visit

There is a secret 'priest hole' at Ripley Castle in North Yorkshire. Several members of the Gunpowder Gang visited the castle.

Becoming a Catholic

Guy became a **Catholic** while he was at St Peter's School in York. At school he was friends with two brothers, John and Christopher Wright. Later, they too took part in the Gunpowder Plot.

Can you find the Wright brothers in this picture of eight members of the Gunpowder Gang?

Three friends of Guy's grew up to be Catholic priests and they were put to death during the **reign** of Elizabeth I. Guy became angry about the way Catholics were being treated in England.

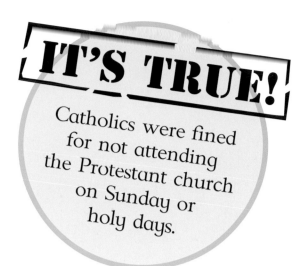

It's true!

Catholics were fined for not attending the Protestant church on Sunday or holy days.

Protestants tortured and killed Catholic priests to try and frighten Catholic families into becoming Protestants.

A brave soldier

When he was twenty-three Guy became a soldier in the Spanish army. Spain was a **Catholic** country and Guy wanted to fight for the Catholic Church.

The king of Spain was Philip II. Guy asked him to help the Catholics in England. Guy was disappointed when the Catholic king refused.

Guy was a brave soldier. He **trained** as a miner and was good at digging tunnels and using **gunpowder**. While he was in Spain, Guy agreed to become involved in a plot to kill King James I.

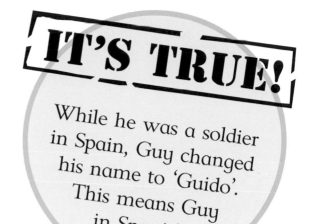

IT'S TRUE!

While he was a soldier in Spain, Guy changed his name to 'Guido'. This means Guy in Spanish.

This engraving shows the Spanish army defeating the Dutch army at the siege of Louvain.

A plot to kill the king

Guy moved back to England in May 1604. He joined a small group of English **Catholics** who wanted to remove the **Protestants** and take over the running of the country. Robert Catesby was the leader of the group.

Robert Catesby's family were Catholics. His father spent much of his life in prison for refusing to become a Protestant.

The thirteen men planned to use **gunpowder** to blow up the **Houses of Parliament**. They chose 5 November 1605 as the day of the explosion because James I would be opening Parliament on that day.

IT'S TRUE!

As part of the plot, Guy Fawkes called himself John Johnson and moved into a house near the Houses of Parliament.

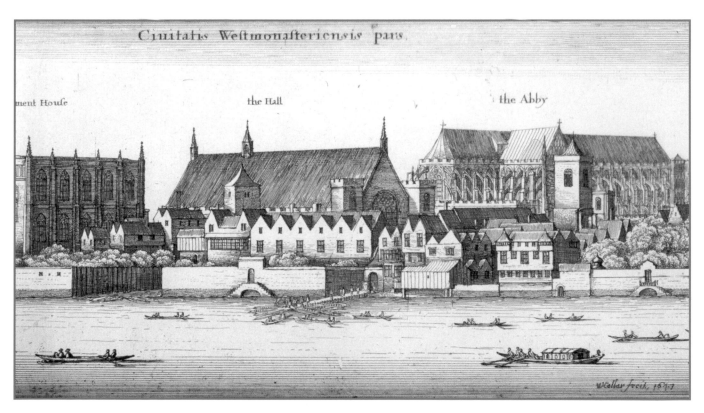

Cuitatis Westmonasteriensis pars.

ment House   the Hall   the Abby

In 1605 the Houses of Parliament was just a few small buildings. It was in a busy area with houses, shops and inns next to it.

Guy's role in the plot

The house where Guy Fawkes was living had a cellar that led right underneath the **Parliament** buildings. The gang hid 36 barrels of **gunpowder** there. It was Guy's job to guard the gunpowder.

a Piece of good underplot

Guy Fawkes had to take great care when he was guarding the gunpowder. A single spark could make it explode.

But news of the secret plot leaked out when a letter was sent to a **Catholic** Minister. It warned him not to attend the opening of Parliament. He was worried and showed the letter to the king.

If you look carefully at this picture from 1647, you can see the **plotters** in the cellar below where King James is sitting, with the **Members of Parliament.**

Caught in the act

On 5 November, the king ordered his soldiers to search the **Houses of Parliament**. They went down into the cellars and found the barrels of **gunpowder** hidden under piles of firewood.

The king's soldiers searched the Houses of Parliament twice before they found Guy Fawkes in the cellar.

When they found Guy Fawkes, he was carrying a lantern and had fuses in his pockets to light the **gunpowder**. When Guy was arrested the other **plotters** left London and went into hiding.

IT'S TRUE!

Each year, at the opening of **Parliament**, special guards search the cellars. This is done in memory of the failed Gunpowder Plot.

This lantern is believed to be the one used by Guy Fawkes. It can be seen in the Ashmolean Museum in Oxford.

Torture and treason

Guy Fawkes was taken to the Tower of London. He signed a **confession** to say he was part of the plot to kill the king. He refused to say who the other **plotters** were. The king ordered that Guy be **tortured** until he named them.

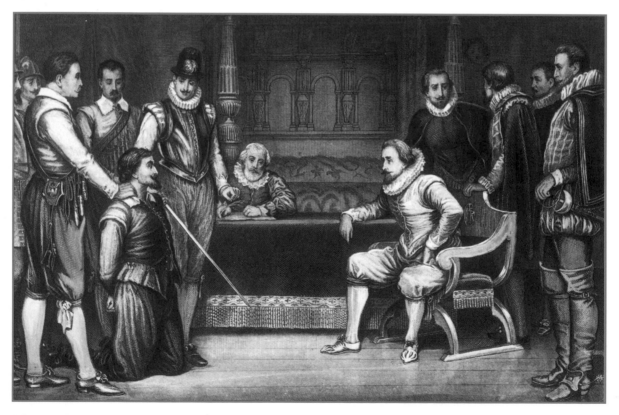

King James I demanded to see Guy Fawkes. He wanted to meet the man who had tried to kill him.

Once Guy had given their names, the other plotters were soon caught. The members of the Gunpowder Plot were tried for **treason** and sentenced to death.

Places to Visit

At the Tower of London there is a plaque telling the story of the Gunpowder Plot in the room where Guy confessed.

Guy Fawkes signed two confessions using the name Guido. His writing is harder to read for the second signature because it was written after he had been tortured.

Remember, remember, the 5ᵗʰ November...

In January 1606 Guy Fawkes was hanged. His body was dragged through the streets and his head was stuck on a pole. It was a warning to other people to never betray their king and country.

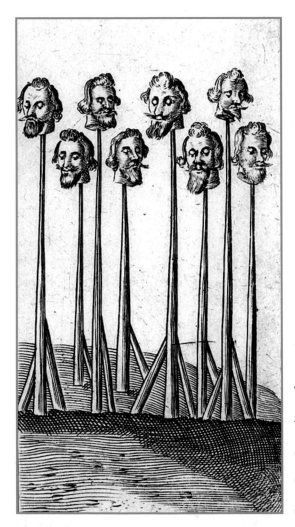

The people of London came to see the gruesome sight of the heads of Guy Fawkes and the other **traitors** stuck on poles.

Every year, on 5 November, we celebrate the failure of the daring plot to kill the king. We light bonfires, just like the people of London did over 400 years ago, when they gave thanks that their king was safe.

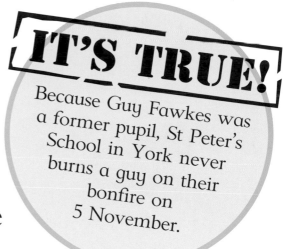

IT'S TRUE!

Because Guy Fawkes was a former pupil, St Peter's School in York never burns a guy on their bonfire on 5 November.

The 'guy' at the front of this bonfire **procession** is meant to be Guy Fawkes. He will be burned on top of a huge bonfire.

Timeline

1532	Henry VIII breaks away from the Catholic religion and makes himself the head of the Church of England
1558	Elizabeth I becomes Queen of England. During her reign she passes laws against Catholics
1570	Guy Fawkes is born into a Protestant family in York on 13 April
1593	Guy Fawkes becomes a soldier in the Spanish Army, fighting for the Catholic Church
1596	Guy Fawkes fights in the Spanish Army at the siege of Calais
1603	Queen Elizabeth I dies
	King James VI of Scotland becomes James I of England. It becomes even more dangerous to be a Catholic in England
1604	Guy Fawkes moves back to England in May and joins the Gunpowder Gang
1605	In March, the plotters store 36 barrels of gunpowder in the cellar under the Houses of Parliament
1605	On 26 October, a secret letter is sent Lord Monteagle warning him not to go to the opening of Parliament
1605	The Gunpowder Plot fails when Guy Fawkes is found under the Parliament buildings on the morning of 5 November
1606	On 31 January, Guy and other members of the Gunpowder Gang are executed for treason

Glossary

Catholics people who believe that the Pope in Rome is the head of their religion

christened a Christian ceremony accepting someone into the Church

confession saying that you have done something wrong

explosives something used for making things blow up

gunpowder a powder which explodes when it is set alight

Houses of Parliament the buildings where the group of people that make the laws of the United Kingdom meet

Member of Parliament a person voted for by the people to represent them in parliament, where laws are agreed upon

plotters a group of people who make a secret plan together

procession a number of people and carriages that travel along a planned route as part of a public festival or occasion

Protestants people who believe that the king or queen is the head of the Church of England

reign the period of time that a king or queen is monarch of their country

tortured to have hurt and punished someone, often to find out information

trained to learn how to do something properly

traitors people who turn against their country and its king or queen

treason a crime against a country or its king or queen

Further information

Books

Beginning History: The Gunpowder Plot by Liz Gogerly (Wayland, 2003)

Guy Fawkes by Richard Brassey (Orion Children's Books, 2005)

Websites

http://www.show.me.uk/gunpowderplot/
Follow the illustrated story of the gunpowder plot.

http://www.historylearningsite.co.uk/gunpowder_plot_of_1605.htm
More detail for teachers and parents, looking at the roles of the members of the gunpowder gang and how it all went wrong.

Index